This Book Belongs to:

....

Authentic

Consultant: Fiona Moss, Asesora RE de RE Today Services
Project Editor: Harriet Stone
Designer: James Handlon

Published by Authentic Media Limited,
PO Box 6326, Bletchley,
Milton Keynes, MK1 9GG

First published in the UK
by QED Publishing, Inc.
Part of The Quarto Group
The Old Brewery, 6 Blundell Street
London, N7 9BH

A catalogue record for this book is available from the British Library.

ISBN: 978 1 86024 999 0

Printed in China

The Stories and Miracles of Jesus

Stories from the New Testament

CONTENTS

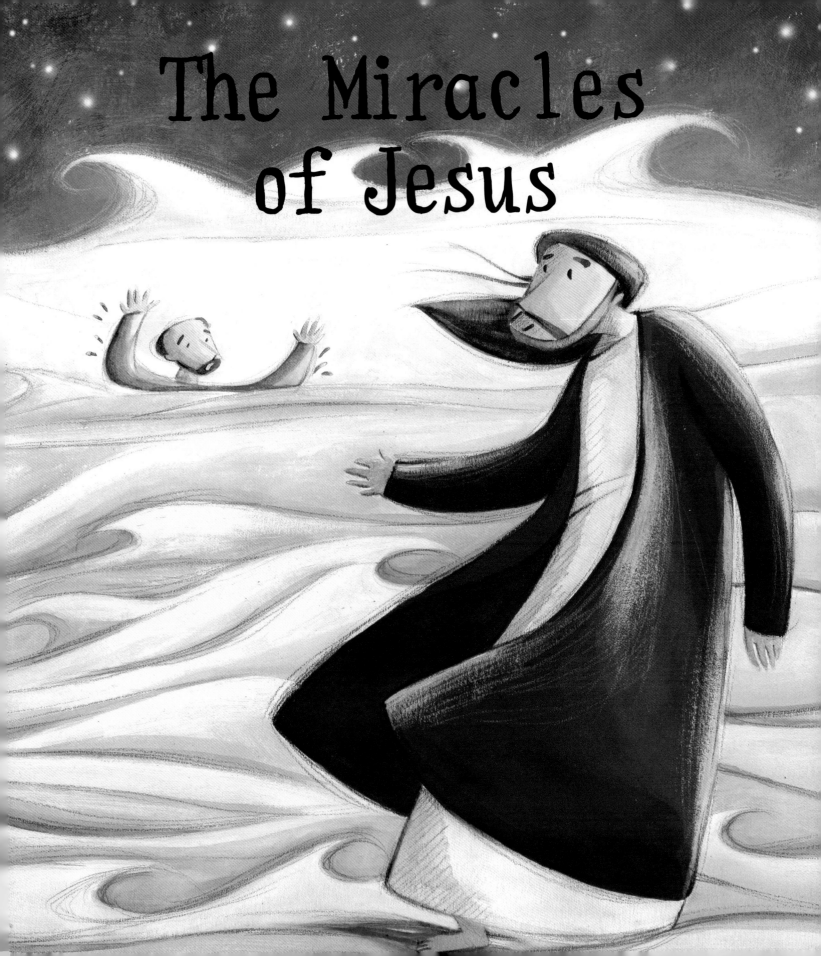

The Miracles
of Jesus

When Jesus was a young man, he travelled from village to village teaching God's message.

Wherever he went, people came to listen to the stories he told.

Soon, lots of people had heard about Jesus. Whenever he arrived in a village, a crowd quickly gathered to meet him.

One day, a big crowd followed Jesus down to the lake. There wasn't enough room for everybody so Jesus asked a man called Peter if he could use his boat.

Peter pushed the boat
a little way into the water.
Now everyone could see and hear Jesus.

While Jesus was teaching the crowd,
the other fishermen were putting
their nets away.

When Jesus had finished, he said to Peter,
"Take the boat out into deep water
and cast your net."

"We fished all night and caught nothing," said Peter. "But if you say so."

Peter sailed to the deepest
part of the lake and
cast his net.

Soon the net was full of fish!
It was so full that the net broke.

Peter called the other
boat over to help.

As they hauled in the fish,
the boats began to sink!

The fishermen couldn't believe how many fish they had caught.

FLIP!

Peter knelt down to thank Jesus, as he didn't think he deserved it. But Jesus said to them, "Follow me, then You'll be fishers of men!"

When they reached the shore, Peter and the other fishermen, Andrew, James and John, left their boats to follow Jesus.

FLOP!

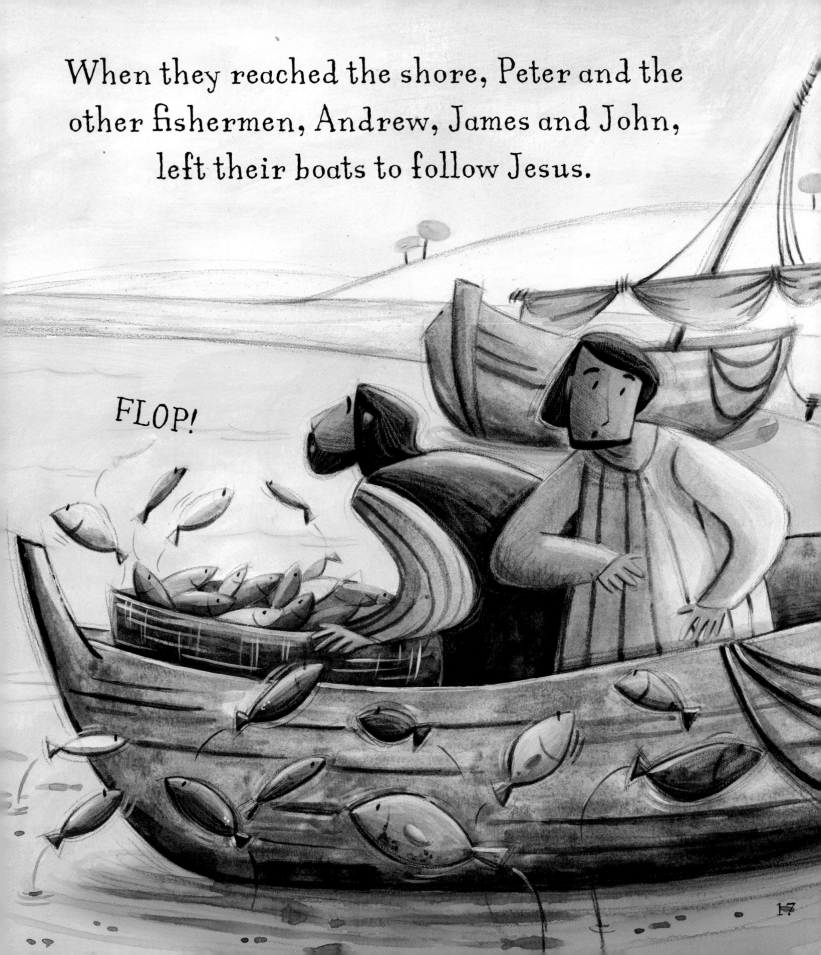

Jesus chose twelve disciples from his many followers:

Andrew,
Peter's brother

Philip

Bartholomew

Peter

James

John,
James's brother

Thomas

Matthew

James, the younger

Thaddaeus

Simon

Judas

"Follow me then you'll be
God's messengers," said Jesus.

19

Jesus loved to teach God's message
and people loved to listen to him.

They followed him everywhere.

But one day, Jesus was sad because
his cousin, John, had died.
Jesus got on a boat
to rest and pray.

When he came back to shore, the people were still waiting for him.

Jesus welcomed them.

He started to teach and heal the sick people.

All day, Jesus spoke to the crowd.
When evening came, the disciples said to Jesus,
"It's late and these people are far from home.
Send them away, to buy some food."

"You can give them some food," replied Jesus.

"That would cost too much!"
the disciples grumbled.

"Go and find out how much food we have,"
Jesus told his disciples.

The disciples went off
among the crowd. They came
back with a boy who had
five loaves and two fish.

24

Jesus told his disciples to sit everyone down in groups. Jesus took the five loaves and two fish and thanked God for the food.

Then he divided the food into baskets
for each of the disciples.

The disciples shared the
food among the people.

Everyone ate as much as they wanted.

CRUNCH!

MUNCH!

YUM!

After everyone had eaten, the disciples collected up the baskets.

When they came back, the twelve baskets were full of food!

They couldn't believe their eyes.

Later, Jesus and his disciples
went down to the lake. They were
going to a town on the other side.

The disciples climbed into
the boat. Jesus stayed behind.

"You go on ahead,"
he told the disciples.
"I have something
I need to do first."

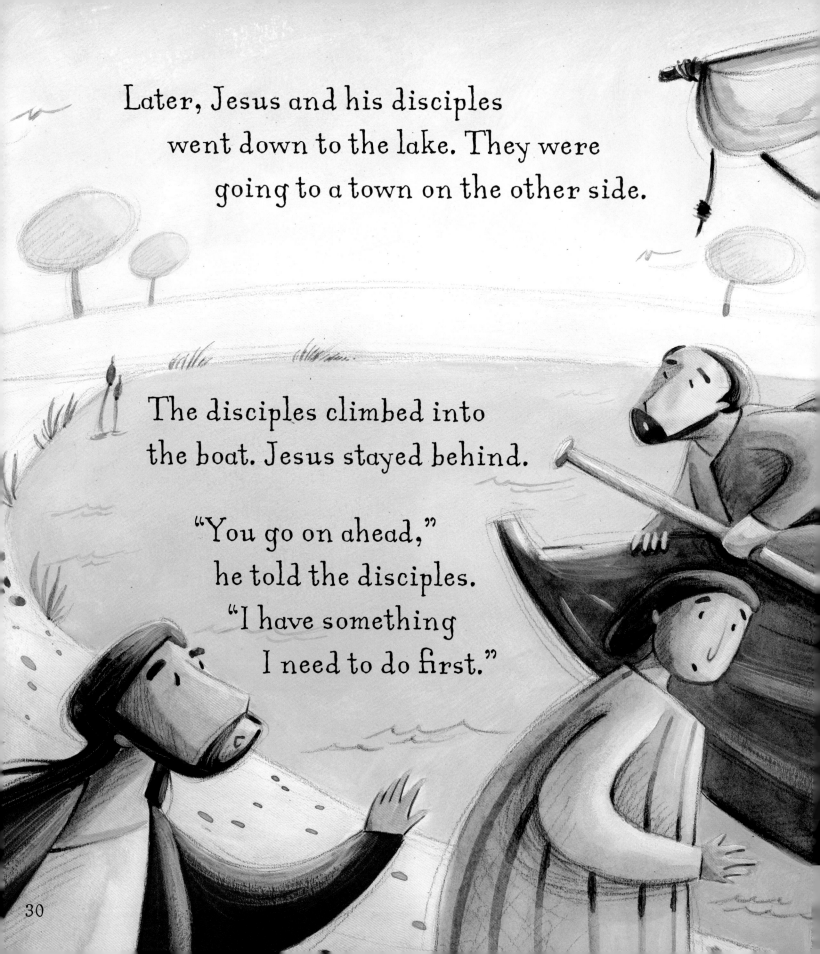

At last, the crowd went home. Jesus sat alone
on the mountain to pray.

Later that night,
Jesus looked out
over the lake.

SPLASH!

CRASH!

The boat was now far from the shore,
tossing this way and that.
The disciples were struggling to row the boat,
fighting against the wind and the waves.

33

It was still dark when the disciples saw
a white figure coming towards them.
They were terrified.

"It's a ghost!" they cried.

But it was Jesus,
walking on the water.

Jesus called to the disciples,
"Be brave! It's only me!"

"Lord, if it's you," Peter replied,
"tell me to come to you on the water."

"Come," Jesus said.

So Peter got out of the boat and
walked on the water towards Jesus.
But he was scared and began to sink.

"Save me!" he cried.

Jesus reached out his hand and caught Peter.
"Did you doubt that God would save you?" Jesus asked.

As they climbed back into the boat,
the wind died down.
The disciples were amazed.

"You really are the Son of God,"
they said to Jesus.

Next Steps

Look back through the story to find more to talk about and join in with.

* Copy the actions. Do the actions with the characters – haul up the fishing nets; put your hands together to pray; row the boat; sink in the water like Peter.

* Join in with the rhyme. Pause to encourage joining in with
  "Follow me, then
  You'll be fishers of men!"
  and
  "Five loaves and two fish.
  It's only enough to fill one dish!"

* Count in fives and twos. Count two fish, two oars, five loaves, five sheep. Count the disciples. Can you name all twelve of them?

* Name the colours. What colours are the fish? What colours are in the boy's hat? Look back to spot the colours on other pages.

* All shapes and sizes. Look for big, middle-size and small baskets, fish and birds.

Now that you've read the story... what do you remember?

* Why did Jesus get into Peter's boat?
* What happened when Peter pulled up his fishing nets?
* Why was Jesus sad?
* What food did the disciples find?
* How many baskets of leftovers were there?
* Who walked on the water?

What does the story tell us?
We should trust in God to give us all we need.

The Good Samaritan

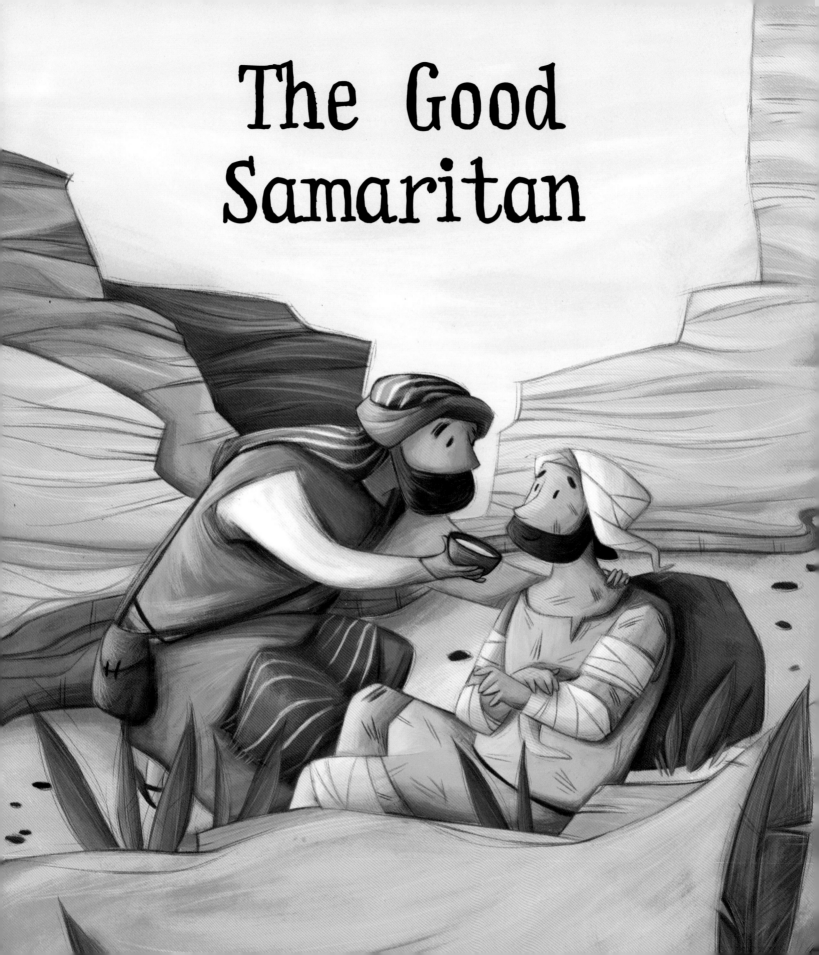

Jesus was a great storyteller. People came from miles around to hear his stories about God and his kingdom.

One day, Jesus told this story, to help people understand how God wanted them to care for one another...

"A man set off down the long road from Jerusalem to Jericho. He left the city and soon he was walking through the lonely hills.

44

The man felt a bit scared among the shadowy cliffs. There might be fierce wild animals living in the rocky caves.

There might be...

"Robbers!

Suddenly, a gang of men jumped out from their hiding place in the rocks.

46

The robbers knocked the
man down. BASH!
They beat him up and stole all he had. Then they
left the poor man lying at the side of the road.

47

"Time passed. The man lay there in the hot sun.

He was thirsty. His head hurt. His cuts
and bumps and bruises were very sore.

The man needed help.
How long would he have to wait?

"At last, the man heard footsteps.

'Help!'

A priest from the temple in Jerusalem came along. Surely this man who taught about God would stop to help?

50

The priest saw the man lying there but didn't go near him.

'Mustn't be late,' he said.
And the priest hurried on his way.

"Later, the man heard more footsteps.

'Help!'

It was someone who helped
the priest in the temple.
Would he have time to stop?

52

He crept closer to look at the man. The man told him he had been attacked by robbers.

'The robbers might still be nearby!' he thought.

And he too went on his way.

Oh dear. It was a foreigner: a man from Samaria.
His people didn't talk to Samaritans.
They didn't like one another.

Why should this
stranger help?

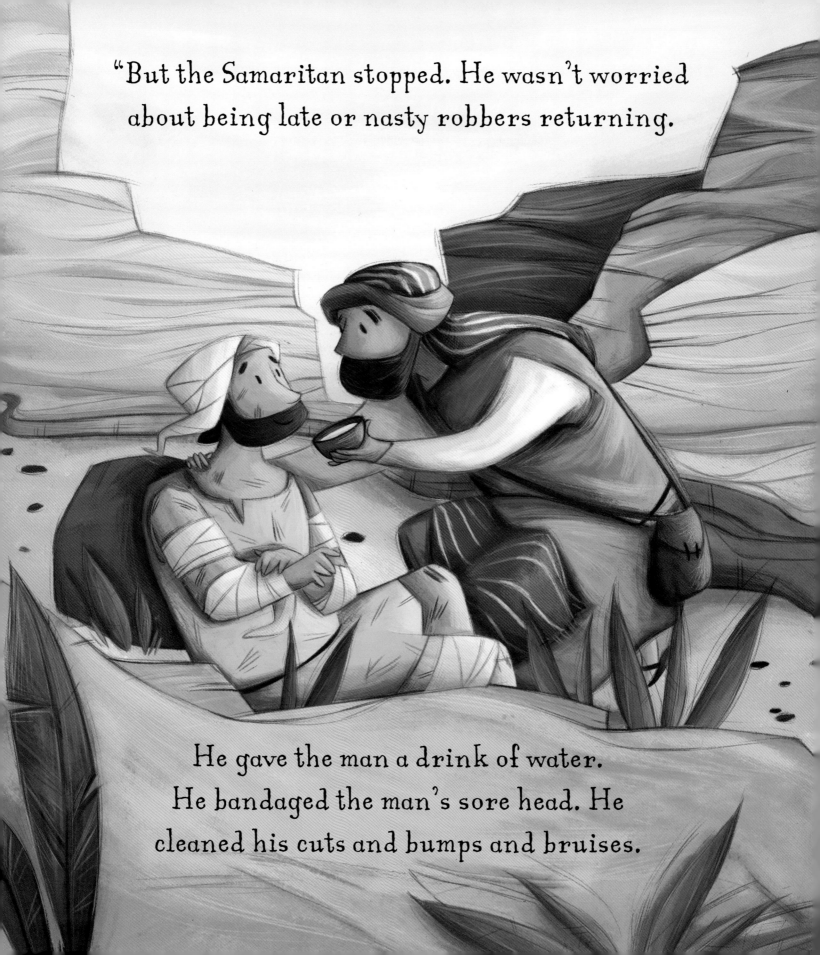

"But the Samaritan stopped. He wasn't worried about being late or nasty robbers returning.

He gave the man a drink of water. He bandaged the man's sore head. He cleaned his cuts and bumps and bruises.

Then he gently lifted him onto his donkey.

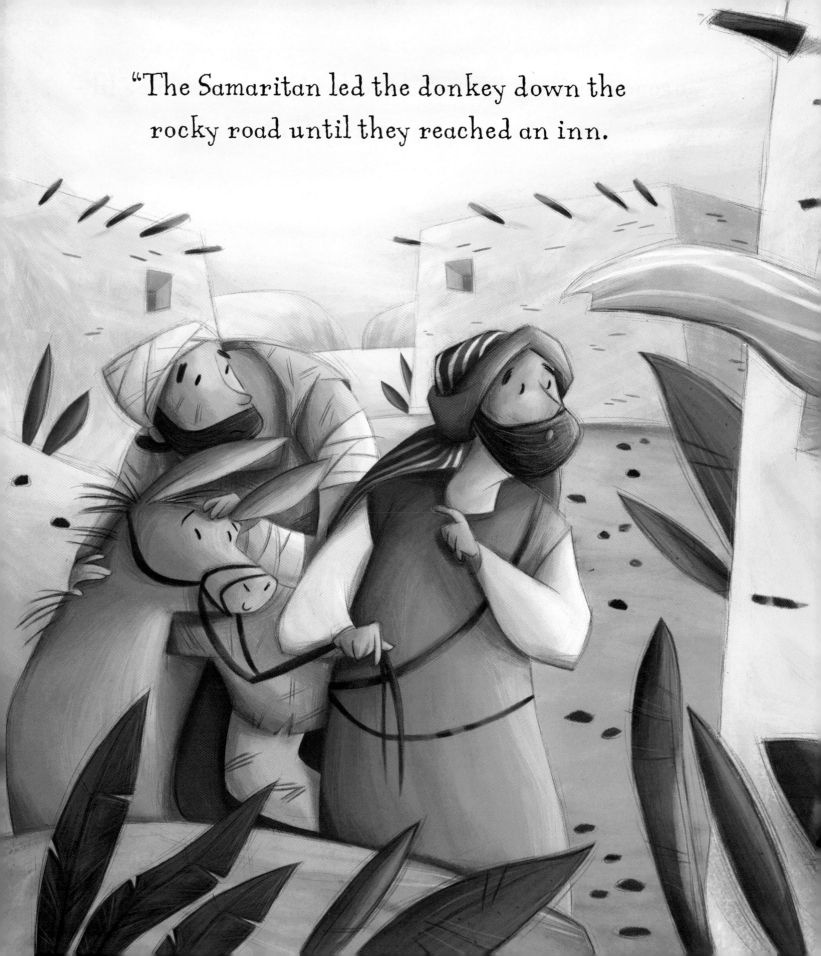

"The Samaritan led the donkey down the rocky road until they reached an inn.

'I need somewhere to care for this poor man,' he told the innkeeper. 'He has been attacked by robbers.'

59

"The next day, the Samaritan gave the innkeeper some money and said:

'Take care of him and let him stay. If you need more, then I will pay.'

Promising he would return,
the Samaritan went on his way."

Jesus looked at the people
listening to his story.

"So which man did what
God wants?" he asked.

"The man who showed kindness," someone answered.

"Now go and do the same," said Jesus. "Show God's love to anyone who needs your help. Even strangers."

63

Next Steps

What does Jesus want us to learn from the story of the Good Samaritan?

Jesus told this story to show how God wants us to treat other people. He wants us to be kind to others and to show love to anyone who needs help, just as the man from Samaria did when he stopped to help the injured foreigner.

You can find this story in Luke 10 in the Bible:

"Love your neighbour as yourself" (Luke 10:27).

Now that you've read the story, here are some things to talk about and join in with.

★ Say the names of some people you love: how have you ever helped them?

★ Have you ever needed help?

★ Were you helped by a person you knew?

★ Does it make a difference whether we know the person we're helping or not?

★ Try to memorize the Samaritan's rhyme:

> "Take care of him and let him stay.
> If you need more, then I will pay."

★ Copy the actions of the characters in the story: pretend to walk down the road; care for the hurt man; pay the innkeeper; wave goodbye.

The Sower

Jesus told stories to explain the message of God.
People liked to listen to them.

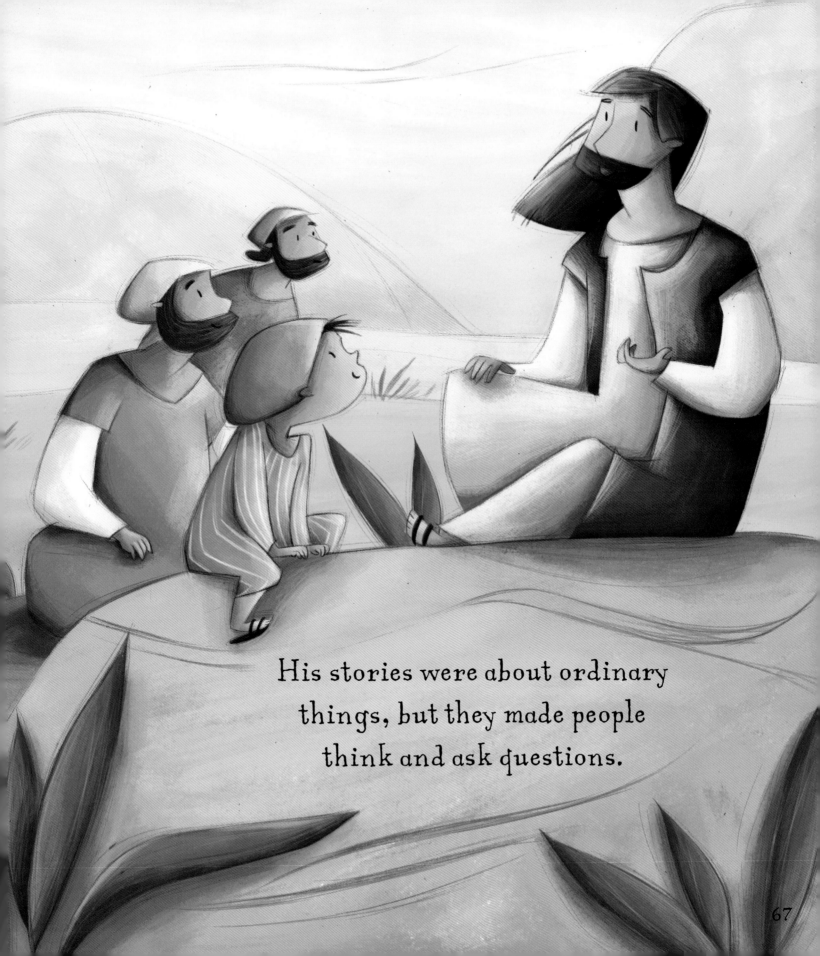

His stories were about ordinary
things, but they made people
think and ask questions.

One day as the crowd listened, Jesus pointed to a farmer in a nearby field.

People turned to look. The man was sowing
seeds as he walked up and down the field.

Jesus told them this
story about a sower...

"One evening, a farmer said, 'The field is ready. It's time to plant my crops.'

Early next morning, he filled a big
bag with grain seeds, slung it over his
shoulder and set off to his field.

"Slowly and steadily, the farmer trudged
up and down the ploughed field.

Handful by handful, he
threw seeds into the air.

Whoosh!

72

Where did the scattered seeds fall?

"Some seeds landed nearby.
Others were carried away by the breeze.

The little seeds fell here and there...
the farmer didn't notice where.

He would find out
when the seeds
grew shoots.

...and then greedy birds swooped down and gobbled them up!

CAW!

CAW!

"Some seeds fell on stony ground.

The seeds began to grow, but they
needed water. Soon their tiny shoots
drooped and died in the hot sun.

Some seeds fell among thorns.
The seeds put down roots and grew
strong shoots. But the thorns were
stronger and choked the little plants.

"But some seeds fell on good rich soil. They made deep roots and grew big green shoots.

The farmer was pleased to see these strong new plants.

80

'Maybe the harvest will
be good,' he said.

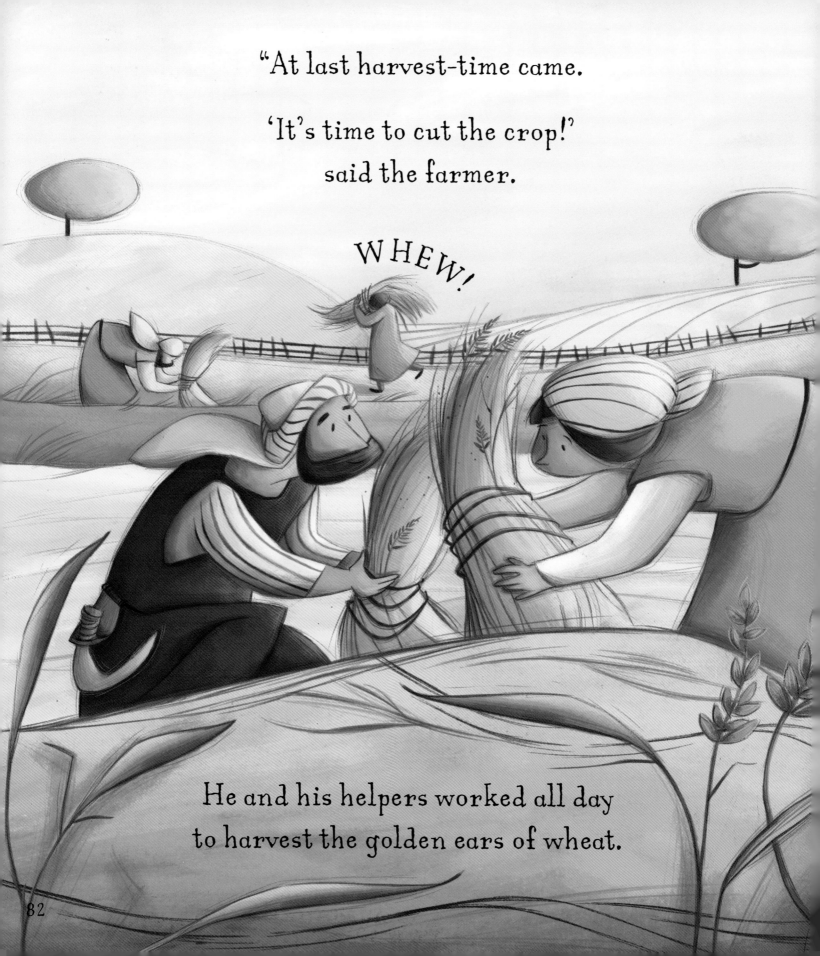

"At last harvest-time came.

'It's time to cut the crop!'
said the farmer.

WHEW!

He and his helpers worked all day
to harvest the golden ears of wheat.

And every plant made lots of new seeds – a hundred times more than the seed the farmer had sown."

"But what does the story mean?"
asked one of Jesus' friends.

"The seeds are what
God tells us about his
kingdom," said Jesus.
"Some people don't really
listen. So God's message
is snatched away, like the
seeds the birds gobbled up.

"Some people are glad to
hear what God tells them.
But as soon as trouble
comes, they are just like
the plants that drooped
and died.

"Some people hear and gladly accept God's teaching. Then their life gets too busy and their understanding does not grow. That's like the seeds that fell among thorns.

"But some people really listen and understand what God wants.

"They are like the seeds that fell on good soil and the plants that made more new seeds.

"They do as God asks and their lives show amazing results."

87

Next Steps

What does Jesus want us to learn from the story of the Sower?

Jesus told this story to show that God wants people to open their hearts to him: to listen carefully to his words, think about what his words really mean and do what he asks. The seeds that fell on good, rich soil and grew well represent people who listen to God and act on his word.

You can find this story in Luke 8 in the Bible:
"The seed is the word of God" (Luke 8:11).

Now that you've read the story, here are some things to talk about and join in with

★ Have you ever planted any seeds? What happened to them?

★ Which seeds in this story grew big and strong?

★ Who did Jesus say the different seeds stood for?

★ What does Jesus want everyone to do?

★ Try to memorize this rhyme: "The little seeds fell here and there...
                    the farmer didn't notice where."

★ Copy the actions of the characters in the story: pretend to walk up and down the field scattering seeds; chase away the greedy birds; help to gather the harvest.

The Lost Sheep

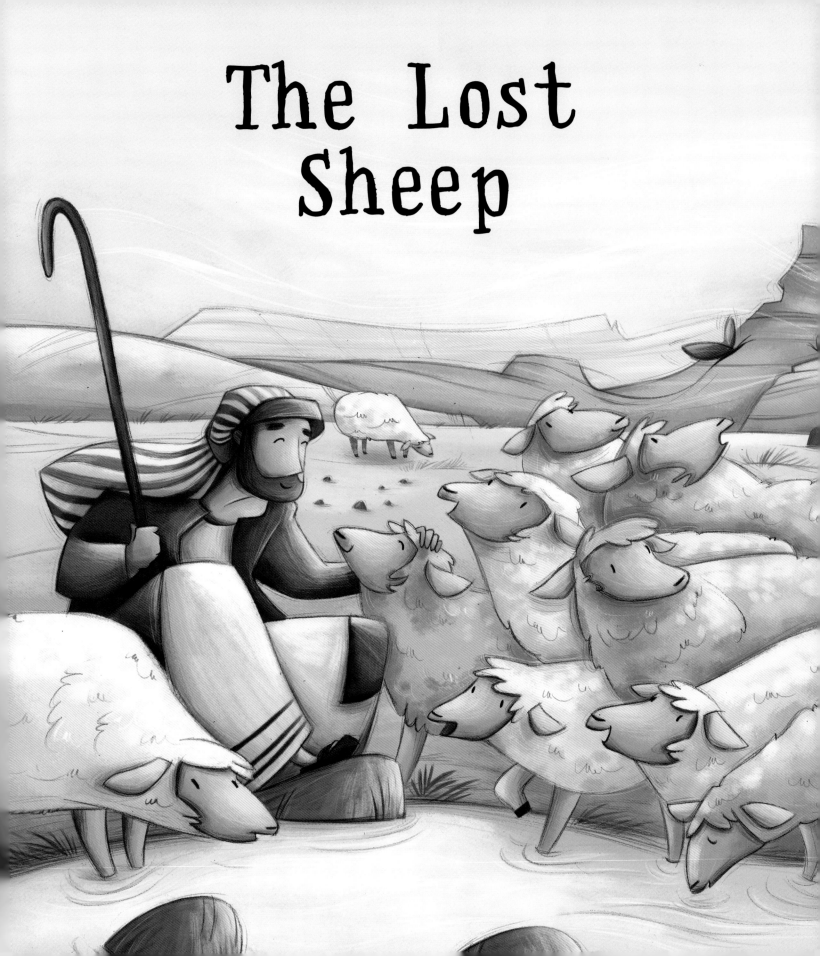

All kinds of people came to listen to Jesus' stories about God's message.

Some were good.
Some were bad. Some were in trouble.

Jesus welcomed everyone.

Some thought Jesus should only be friends with good people.

One man asked, "Why do you spend so much time with bad people?"

Jesus told this story to explain...

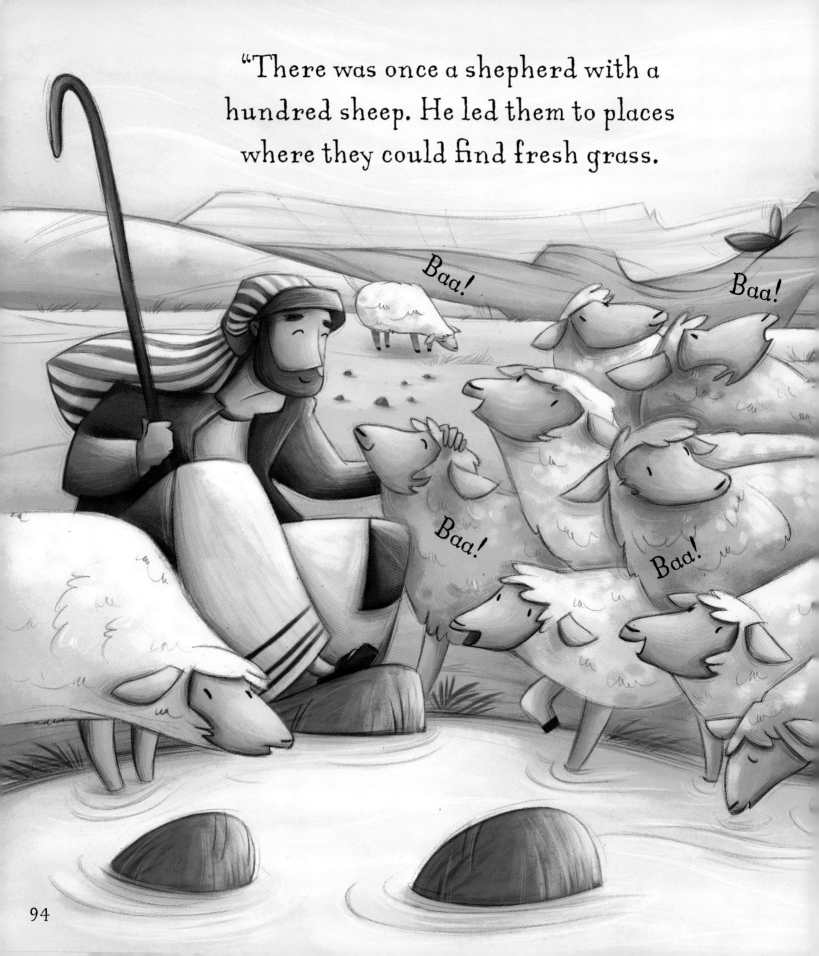

"There was once a shepherd with a hundred sheep. He led them to places where they could find fresh grass.

94

He made sure they always found water
to drink. He took great care of his flock.

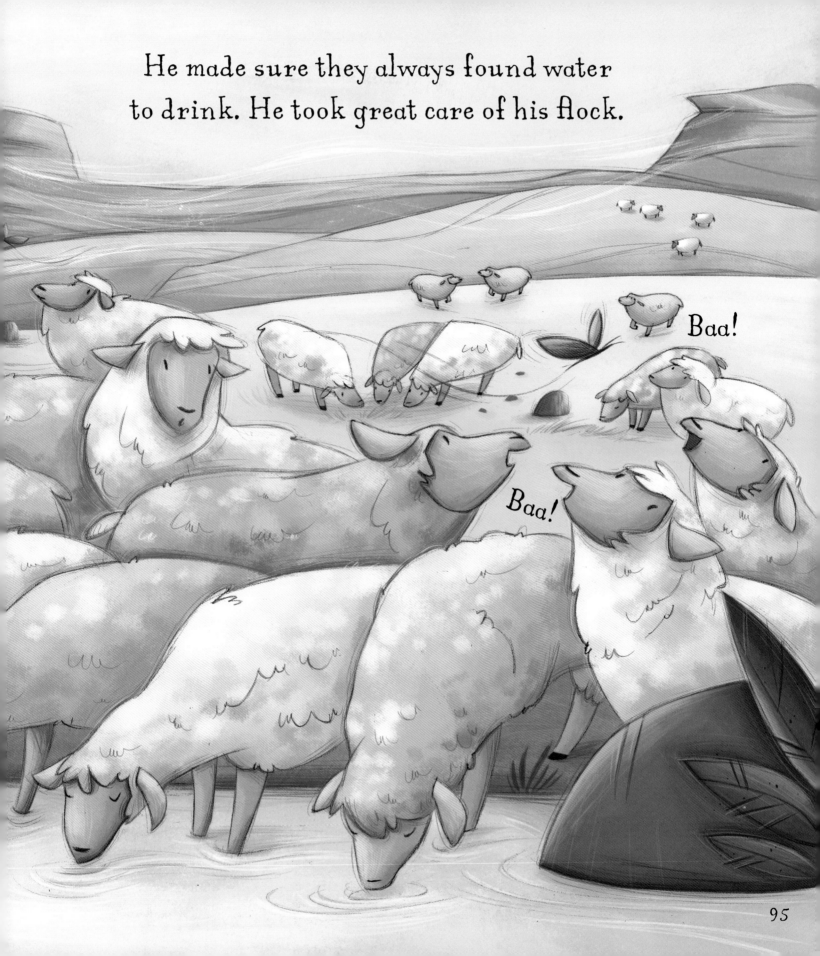

"Every night, the shepherd counted all the sheep, making sure they were safe.

One night, he counted, as usual – all
the way from one to ninety-nine.

But the last sheep was missing!

"One sheep must have wandered away and got lost.

The shepherd cared for the missing sheep as much as for the rest. He had to try to find the one that was lost.

98

He knew the ninety-nine sheep
would be safe together. So he set
out to look for the lost sheep.

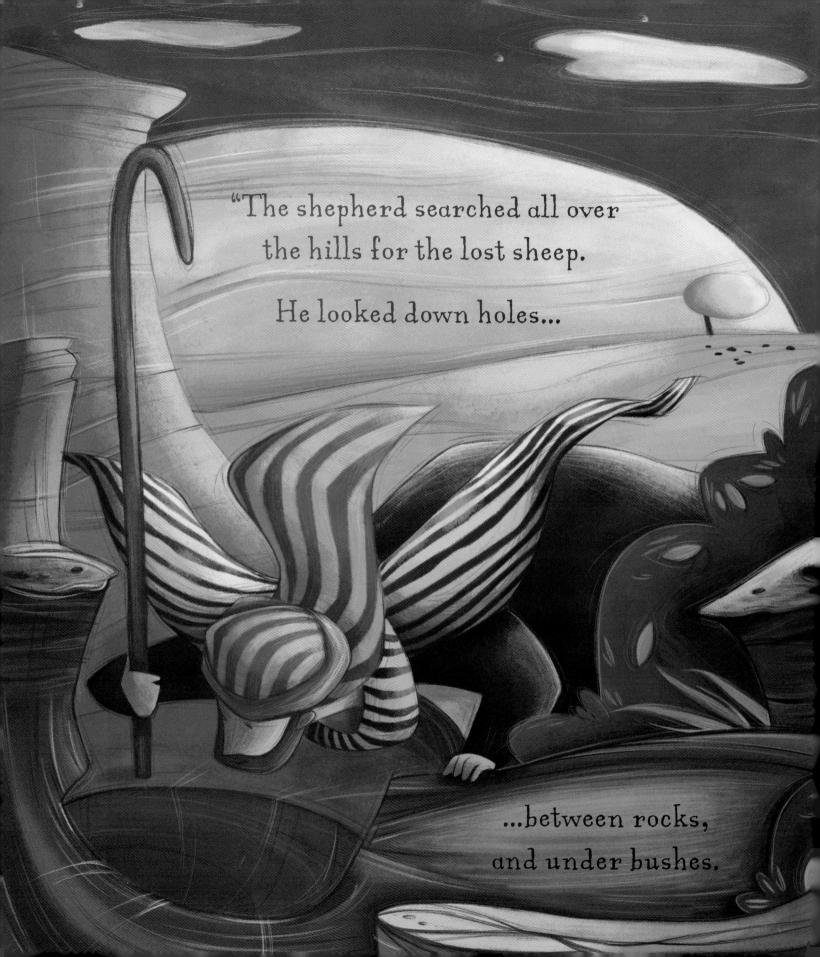

"The shepherd searched all over the hills for the lost sheep.

He looked down holes...

...between rocks, and under bushes.

Time passed and he didn't hear a bleat or a baa.

But the shepherd did not give up.

"At last, he heard a tiny sound.

He followed the sound.
It grew louder.

BAA!

And there was the missing sheep!

103

"The shepherd was very happy.

He gently picked the sheep up.
He put it across his shoulders.

And he carried it all the way home.

"Then the shepherd called out to his friends:
'My sheep went astray and lost its way.
But now it's here, let's raise a cheer!'"

And they all had a party to celebrate."

"When you lose something precious,
aren't you pleased to find it?"
Jesus asked the people listening to him.

"That's just like God," he said.

"And that's why I spend time with
people who have taken the wrong path
and those who are in trouble."

"God is like the shepherd in this story.
And we are all his sheep.

"When someone comes back to God, he is overjoyed. He doesn't want anyone to be lost."

Next Steps

What does Jesus want us to learn from the story of the Lost Sheep?

Jesus wants people to understand God's love: he never gives up on people and is overjoyed when anyone in trouble comes back to him, just as the shepherd was overjoyed when he found his missing sheep.

You can find this story in Matthew 18 and Luke 15 in the Bible:
"There will be joy in heaven when someone comes back to God" (Luke 15:7).

Now that you've read the story, here are some things to talk about and join in with

★ How many sheep were in the shepherd's flock?

★ What did the shepherd do to care for his sheep?

★ Why did the shepherd want to find the lost sheep?

★ How did the shepherd take the sheep home?

★ Why did the shepherd have a party?

★ Try to memorize the shepherd's rhyme: "My sheep went astray and lost its way.
But now it's here, let's raise a cheer!"

★ Copy the actions of the shepherd: pretend to count the flock; search for the lost sheep; carry the sheep on your shoulders

The Two Houses

Jesus was a great storyteller.
But he wanted people to understand
that listening to his words wasn't enough.

They also had to do what he told them.

So Jesus told them this story.

"One day, a man decided to build a house.

116

'I've planned every detail,' he told his friend.

First, he bought a plot
of hard rocky ground.

He dug deep into the earth above the rock.

It was hard work.

It was
hot work.

'A well-built house needs firm foundations,' he told his friend.

The man made sure he built
everything just right.

120

He was very pleased when at last
the house on the rock was finished.

Everyone admired the house.

His friend even decided to build a new home of his own.
'There must be an easier place to build,' he thought.

His friend bought a plot of ground near the river.
It was soft and sandy and easy to dig.

'Building really
isn't such hard work,'
he thought.

Before long he, too, had finished building his house.

The two men were pleased
with their fine new homes.

Now they could enjoy the summer weather. And when winter came, the houses would keep them cosy and dry.

One day, dark clouds filled the sky.
Wind began to blow.

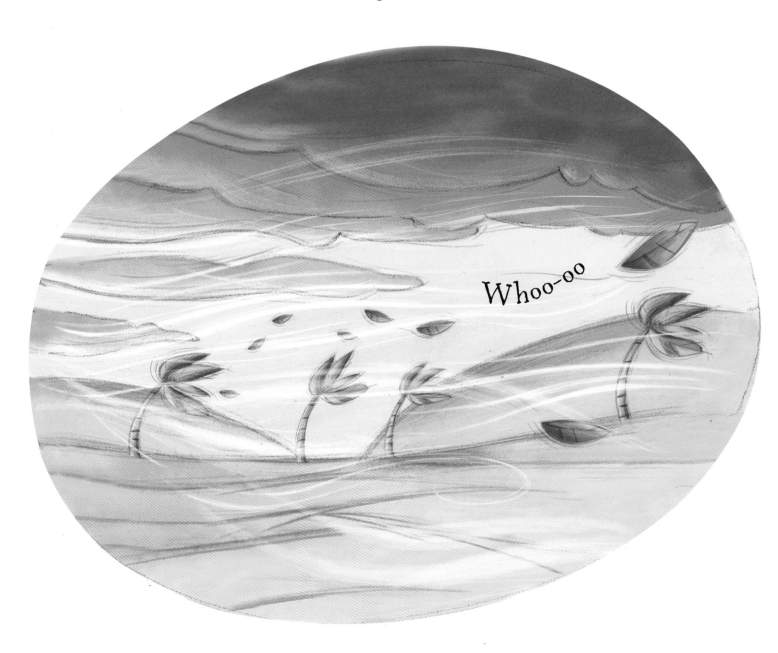

Rain fell, faster and faster.

Plip! Plop!

Water splashed over the sand.

Whenever wind whistled through the windows the house built on rock stood firm.

The house built on sand shook and shifted.
Its wobbly walls crumbled and lifted...

...until with a CRASH and a SPLASH the house built on sand fell down flat!"

Jesus looked at the people listening to his story.

"My words are like that rock," said Jesus.

"If you build your life on them you will stand firm too, as firm as the house on the rock."

Next Steps

What does Jesus want us to learn from the story of the Two Houses?

Jesus told this story to show how important it is to follow his example. Listening to his words and living God's way gives firm foundations for how to live, just as the rock provided strong foundations for the house.

You can find this story in Matthew 7 and Luke 6 in the Bible:
"Therefore everyone who hears these words of mine and puts them into practice is like a wise man who built his house on the rock" (Matthew 7:24).

Now that you've read the story, here are some things to talk about and join in with.

* Have you ever built anything? What did you use? How long did your creation last?
* How do you think builders decide where to build a house?
* Why is rock good to build on?
* What does Jesus want people to build their lives on?
* Try to memorize the rhyme: "The house built on sand shook and shifted.
  Its wobbly walls crumbled and lifted ..."

* Copy the actions of the two men: pretend to dig; lay bricks; pick leaves; try to keep dry in the rain and rising water.